The Lives of Adam and Eve

By Moses

Copyright © 2019 Lamp of Trismegistus. All rights reserved. No part of this publication may be reproduced or transmitted in any form or by any means, electronic or mechanical, including photocopying, recording, or by any information storage and retrieval system, without permission in writing from Lamp of Trismegistus. Reviewers may quote brief passages.

ISBN: 978-1-63118-414-7

Christian Apocrypha Series

Other Books in this Series and Related Titles

The First and Second Gospels of the Infancy of Jesus Christ by Thomas and James (978-1-63118-415-4)

The Book of the Watchers by Enoch
(978-1-63118-416-1)

Lost Chapters of the Book of Daniel and Related Writings by Daniel
(978-1-63118-417-8)

Symbolism of the Corner Stone, the North East Corner and the Religious & Masonic Symbolism of Stones by Albert G. Mackey, William Harvey and William Wynn Westcott
(978-1-63118-412-3)

Ancient Mysteries and Secret Societies by Manly P. Hall
(978-1-63118-410-9)

The Influence of Pythagoras on Freemasonry, the Golden Verses of Pythagoras and the Life and Philosophy of Pythagoras by Albert G. Mackey and Manly P. Hall (978-1-63118-320-1)

The Philosophy of Masonry in Five Parts by Roscoe Pound
(978-1-63118-004-0)

Rosicrucian and Masonic Origins by Manly P. Hall
(978-1-63118-000-2)

The Story and Legend of Hiram Abiff by William Harvey, Manly P. Hall and Albert G. Mackey
(978-1-63118-411-6)

Four Lesser Known Masonic Essays by Frank C. Higgins
(978-1-63118-003-3)

Audio Versions are also Available on Audible and iTunes

Table of Contents

Introduction...7

Prologue...9

The Lives of Adam and Eve...11

Introduction

The Apocrypha are a loosely knit series of books, written by early vanguards of Christianity (covering the eras of both the old and new testaments), and which comprise somewhere between about a dozen to several hundred titles, depending on whom you ask and how that person defines "Apocrypha." A small selection of these can still be found included in the Catholic bible, while a majority of the books in question, were abandoned by church officials in the early centuries of Christianity. Many of these apocryphal books were originally considered canon by early followers of Christ, in the first four centuries following his birth. It wasn't until the meeting of the Council of Nicaea in 325, that Emperor Constantine and a group of roughly 300 church bishops, gathered together with the goal of defining, standardizing and unifying an otherwise splintering Christianity, that many of these writings ceased to be included in the newly established canon. Enjoy then, this book as an example, of just one of the many books of the Christian Apocrypha, and be sure to check out other titles in this series.

Prologue

The Lives of Adam and Eve belongs to a class of Apocrypha which could be described as books written, or claimed to have been written, before the time of Christ, as part of the Old Testament and which frequently contain prophecies. That is to say, they must have originally been Jewish works, and were told probably with no intention to deceive. Jewish legends about Adam were numerous and very old, and the Jewish literary custom of writing ethical works in the form of a survey of history was well established. Later, during the Christian ages, these old legends and prophecies of Adam were gathered into a single book, a Latin tome entitled "*The Lives of Adam and Eve.*" During the fourteenth and fifteenth centuries this text was translated into almost every European tongue and was immensely popular. The book itself chronicles events in the life of the couple, following their expulsion from the Garden of Eden until the death of both of them, nine hundred thirty years later. While the text is traditionally ascribed to Moses, the real Jewish origins of this work are no longer known, but the date of their composition must have been somewhere during the very earliest Christian centuries (likely around 100 A.D.), for the tone of the "*Lives of Adam and Eve*" echoes the Jewish religious views of that date, with occasional Christian additions. And, although the original author of this text has been lost to time; we most certainly know that scholar R. H. Charles prepared this translation in 1913.

The Lives of Adam and Eve

Chapter I

When they were driven out from paradise, they made themselves a booth, and spent seven days mourning and lamenting in great grief.

Chapter II

But after seven days, they began to be hungry and started to look for victual to eat, and they found it not. Then Eve said to Adam: "My lord, I am hungry. Go, look for something for us to eat. Perchance the Lord God will look back and pity us and recall us to the place in which we were before."

Chapter III

And Adam arose and walked seven days over all that land, and found no victual such as they used to have in paradise. And Eve said to Adam: "Wilt thou slay me? that I may die, and perchance God the Lord will bring thee into paradise, for on my account hast thou been driven thence." Adam answered: "Forbear, Eve, from such words, that peradventure God bring not some other curse upon us. How is it possible that I should stretch forth my hand against my own flesh? Nay, let us arise and look for something for us to live on, that we fail not."

Chapter IV

And they walked about and searched for nine days, and they found none such as they were used to have in paradise, but found only animals' food. And Adam said to Eve: "This hath the Lord provided for animals and brutes to eat; but we used to have angels' food. But it is just and right that we lament before the sight of God who made us. Let us repent with a great penitence: perchance the Lord will be gracious to us and will pity us and give us a share of something for our living."

Chapter V

And Eve said to Adam: "What is penitence? Tell me, what sort of penitence am I to do? Let us not put too great a labor on ourselves, which we can not endure, so that the Lord will not harken to our prayers: and will turn away His countenance from us, because we have not fulfilled what we promised. My lord, how much penitence hast thou thought to do, for I have brought trouble and anguish upon thee?"

Chapter VI

And Adam said to Eve: "Thou canst not do so much as I, but do only so much as thou hast strength for. For I will spend forty days fasting, but do thou arise and go to the River Tigris and lift up a stone and stand on it in the water up to thy neck in the deep of the river. And let no speech proceed out of thy mouth, since we are unworthy to address the Lord, for our lips are unclean from the unlawful and forbidden tree. And do thou stand in the water of the river thirty-seven days. But I will spend forty days in the water of Jordan, perchance the Lord God will take pity upon us."

Chapter VII

And Eve walked to the River Tigris and did as Adam had told her. Likewise, Adam walked to the River Jordan and stood on a stone up to his neck in water.

Chapter VIII

And Adam said: "I tell thee, water of Jordan, grieve with me, and assemble to me all swimming creatures, which are in thee, and let them surround me and mourn in company with me. Not for themselves let them lament, but for me; for it is not they that have sinned, but I.

"Forthwith, all living things came and surrounded him, and, from that hour the water of the Jordan stood still and its current was stayed."

Chapter IX

And eighteen days passed by; then Satan was wroth and transformed himself into the brightness of angels, and went away to the River Tigris to Eve, and found her weeping, and the devil himself pretended to grieve with her, and he began to weep and said to her: "Come out of the river and lament no more. Cease now from sorrow and moans. Why art thou anxious and thy husband Adam? The Lord God hath heard your groaning and hath accepted your penitence, and all we angels have entreated on your behalf, and made supplication to the Lord; and he hath sent me to bring you out of the water and give you the nourishment which you had in paradise, and for which you are crying out. Now come out of the water and I will conduct you to the place where your victual hath been made ready."

Chapter X

But Eve heard and believed and went out of the water of the river, and her flesh was trembling like grass, from the chill of the water. And when she had gone out, she fell on the earth and the devil raised her up and led her to Adam. But when Adam had seen her and the devil with her, he wept and cried aloud and said: "O Eve, Eve, where is the labor of thy penitence? How hast thou been again ensnared by our adversary, by whose means we have been estranged from our abode in paradise and spiritual joy?"

Chapter XI

And when she heard this, Eve understood that it was the devil who had persuaded her to go out of the river; and she fell on her face on the earth, and her sorrow and groaning and wailing were redoubled. And she cried out and said: "Woe unto thee, thou devil. Why dost thou attack us for no cause? What hast thou to do with us? What have we done to thee? for thou pursuest us with craft. Or why doth thy malice assail us? Have we taken away thy glory and caused thee to be without honor? Why dost thou harry us, thou enemy, and persecute us to the death in wickedness and envy?"

Chapter XII

The Fall of the Devil

And with a heavy sigh, the devil spake: "O Adam! all my hostility, envy, and sorrow is for thee, since it is for thee that I have been expelled from my glory, which I possessed in the heavens in the midst of the angels, and for thee was I cast out in the earth." Adam answered, "What dost thou tell me? What have I done to thee or what is my fault against thee? Seeing that thou hast received no harm or injury from us, why dost thou pursue us?"

Chapter XIII

The devil replied, "Adam, what dost thou tell me? It is for thy sake that I have been hurled from that place. When thou wast formed, I was hurled out of the presence of God and banished from the company of the angels. When God blew into thee the breath of life and thy face and likeness was made in the image of God, Michael also brought thee and made us worship thee in the sight of God; and God the Lord spake: Here is Adam. I have made thee in our image and likeness."

Chapter XIV

And Michael went out and called all the angels saying: "Worship the image of God as the Lord God hath commanded."

And Michael himself worshiped first; then he called me and said: "Worship the image of God the Lord." And I answered, "I have no need to worship Adam." And since Michael kept urging me to worship, I said to him, "Why dost thou urge me? I will not worship an inferior and younger being than I. I am his senior in the Creation, before he was made was I already made. It is his duty to worship me."

Chapter XV

When the angels, who were under me, heard this, they refused to worship him. And Michael saith, "Worship the image of God, but if thou wilt not worship him the Lord God will be wroth with thee." And I said, " If He be wroth with me, I will set my seat above the stars of heaven and will be like the Highest."

Chapter XVI

"And God the Lord was wroth with me and banished me and my angels from our glory; and on thy account were we expelled from our abodes into this world and hurled on the earth. And straightway we were overcome with grief, since we had been spoiled of so great glory. And we were grieved when we saw thee in such joy and luxury. And with guile I cheated thy wife and caused thee to be expelled through her doing from thy joy and luxury, as I have been driven out of my glory."

Chapter XVII

When Adam heard the devil say this, he cried out and wept, and spake: "O Lord my God, my life is in thy hands. Banish this Adversary far from me, who seeketh to destroy my soul, and give me his glory which he himself hath lost." And at that moment the devil vanished before him. But Adam endured in his penance, standing for forty days on end in the water of Jordan.

Chapter XVIII

Cain and Abel

And Eve said to Adam: "Live thou, my lord, to thee life is granted, since thou hast committed neither the first nor the second error. But I have erred and been led astray, for I have not kept the commandment of God; and now banish me from the light of thy life and I will go to the sunsetting, and there will I be, until I die." And she began to walk toward the western parts and to mourn and to weep bitterly and groan aloud. And she made there a booth, while she had in her womb offspring of three months old.

Chapter XIX

And when the time of her bearing approached, she began to be distressed with pains, and she cried aloud to the Lord and said: "Pity me, O Lord; assist me." And she was not heard, and the mercy of God did not encircle her. And she said to herself: "Who shall tell my lord Adam? I implore you, ye luminaries of heaven, what time ye return to the east, bear a message to my lord Adam."

Chapter XX

But in that hour Adam said: "The complaint of Eve hath come to me. Perchance, once more hath the serpent fought with her."

And he went and found her in great distress. And Eve said: "From the moment I saw thee, my lord, my grief-laden soul was refreshed. And now entreat the Lord God on my behalf to harken unto thee and look upon me and free me from my awful pains." And Adam entreated the Lord for Eve.

Chapter XXI

And behold, there came twelve angels and two "virtues," standing on the right and on the left of Eve; and Michael was standing on the right; and he stroked her on the face as far as to the breast, and said to Eve: "Blessed art thou, Eve, for Adam's sake. Since his prayers and intercessions are great, I have been sent that thou mayest receive our help. Rise up now, and prepare thee to bear." And she bore a son and he was shining; and at once the babe rose up and ran and bore a blade of grass in his hands, and gave it to his mother, and his name was called Cain.

Chapter XXII

And Adam carried Eve and the boy and led them to the East. And the Lord God sent divers seeds by Michael the archangel and gave to Adam and showed him how to work and till the ground, that they might have fruit by which they and all their generations might live.

For thereafter Eve conceived and bare a son, whose name was Abel; and Cain and Abel used to stay together.

And Eve said to Adam: "My lord, while I slept, I saw a vision, as it were the blood of our son Abel in the hand of Cain, who was gulping it down in his mouth. Therefore I have sorrow."

And Adam said, "Alas if Cain slew Abel. Yet let us separate them from each other mutually, and let us make for each of them separate dwellings."

Chapter XXIII

And they made Cain an husbandman, but Abel they made a shepherd; in order that in this wise they might be mutually separated. And thereafter, Cain slew Abel, but Adam was then one hundred and thirty years old, but Abel was slain when he was one hundred and twenty-two years.

And thereafter Adam knew his wife and he begat a son and called his name Seth.

Chapter XXIV

And Adam said to Eve, "Behold, I have begotten a son, in place of Abel, whom Cain slew." And after Adam had begotten Seth, he lived eight hundred years more and begat thirty sons and thirty daughters; in all sixty-three children. And they were increased over the face of the earth in their nations.

Chapter XXV

The Vision of Adam

And Adam said to Seth, " Hear, my son, Seth, that I may relate to thee what I heard and saw after your mother and I had been driven out of paradise. When we were at prayer, there came to me Michael the archangel, a messenger of God. And I saw a chariot like the wind, and its wheels were fiery, and I was caught up into the paradise of righteousness, and I saw the Lord sitting and his face was flaming fire that could not be endured. And many thousands of angels were on the right and left of that chariot.

Chapter XXVI

When I saw this I was confounded, and terror seized me, and I bowed myself down before God with my face to the earth. And God said to me, "Behold thou diest, since thou hast transgressed the commandment of God, for thou didst harken rather to the voice of thy wife, whom I gave into thy power, that thou mightest; hold her to thy will. Yet thou didst listen to her and didst pass by My words."

Chapter XXVII

And when I heard these words of God, I fell prone on the earth and worshiped the Lord and said, "My Lord, All powerful and merciful God, Holy and Righteous One, let not the name that is mindful of Thy majesty be blotted out, but convert my soul, for I die and my breath will go out of my mouth. Cast me not out from Thy presence, me whom Thou didst form of the clay of the earth. Do not banish from Thy favor him whom Thou didst nourish."

And lo! a word concerning thee came upon me, and the Lord said to me, "Since thy days were fashioned, thou hast been created with a love of knowledge; therefore there shall not be taken from thy seed forever the right to serve Me."

Chapter XXVIII

And when I heard these words, I threw myself on the earth and adored the Lord God, and said, "Thou art the eternal and supreme God; and all creatures give Thee honor and praise.

"Thou art the true Light gleaming above all lights, the Living Life, infinite mighty Power. To Thee, the spiritual powers give honor and praise. Thou workest on the race of men the abundance of Thy mercy."

After I had worshiped the Lord, straightway Michael, God's archangel, seized my hand and cast me out of the paradise of "vision" and of God's command. And Michael held a rod in his hand, and he touched the waters, which were round about paradise, and they froze hard.

Chapter XXIX

And I went across, and Michael the archangel went across with me, and he led me back to the place whence he had caught me up. Harken, my son Seth, even to the rest of the secrets and sacraments that shall be, which were revealed to me, when I had eaten of the tree of knowledge, and knew and perceived what will come to pass in this age; what God intends to do to His creation of the race of men. The Lord will appear in a flame of fire, and from the mouth of His majesty He will give commandments and statutes; from His mouth will proceed a two-edged sword; and they will sanctify Him in the house of the habitation of His majesty. And He will show them the marvelous place of His majesty. And then they will build a house to the Lord their God in the land which He shall prepare for them, and there they will transgress His statutes and their sanctuary will be burnt up, and their land will be deserted, and they themselves will be dispersed; because they have kindled the wrath of God. And once more he will cause them to come back from their dispersion; and again they will build the house of God; and in the last time the house of God will be exalted greater than of old. And once more iniquity will exceed righteousness. And thereafter God will dwell with men on earth in visible form; and then righteousness will begin to shine. And the house of God will be honored in the age, and their enemies will no more be able to hurt the men, who are believing in God; and God will stir up for Himself a faithful people, whom He shall save for eternity, and the impious shall be punished by God their king, the men who refused to love His law. Heaven and earth, nights and days, and all creatures shall obey Him, and not overstep His commandment. Men shall not change their works, but they shall be changed from forsaking the law of the Lord. Therefore the Lord shall repel from Himself the wicked, and the just shall shine like the sun, in the sight of God. And in that time shall men be purified by water from their sins. But those who are unwilling to be purified by water shall be condemned. And happy shall the man be who hath ruled his soul, when the Judgment shall come to pass and the greatness of God be seen among men and their deeds be inquired into by God, the just judge.

Chapter XXX

The Death of Adam

After Adam was nine hundred and thirty years old, since he knew that his days were coming to an end, he said: "Let all my sons assemble themselves to me, that I may bless them before I die, and speak with them."

And they were assembled in three parts, before his sight, in the house of prayer, where they used to worship the Lord God. And they asked him, saying: "What concerns thee, father, that thou shouldest assemble us, and why dost thou lie on thy bed?" Then Adam answered and said: "My sons, I am sick and in pain." And all his sons said to him: "What does it mean, father, this illness and pain?"

Chapter XXXI

Then said Seth, his son: "O my lord, perchance thou hast longed after the fruit of paradise, which thou wast wont to eat, and therefore thou liest in sadness? Tell me and I will go to the nearest gates of paradise and put dust on my head and throw myself down on the earth before the gates of paradise and lament and make entreaty to God with loud lamentation; perchance he will harken to me and send his angel to bring me the fruit, for which thou hast longed."

Adam answered and said: "No, my son, I do not long for this, but I feel weakness and great pain in my body." Seth answered, "What is pain, my lord father? I am ignorant; but hide it not from us, but tell us about it."

Chapter XXXII

And Adam answered and said: "Hear me, my sons. When God made us, me and your mother, and placed us in paradise and gave us every tree bearing fruit to eat, he laid a prohibition on us concerning the tree of knowledge of good and evil, which is in the midst of paradise; saying, 'Do not eat of it.' But God gave a part of paradise to me and a part to your mother: the trees of the eastern part and north, which is over against Aquilo, he gave to me, and to your mother he gave the part of the south and the western part.

Chapter XXXIII

Moreover God the Lord gave us two angels to guard us. The hour came when the angels had ascended to worship in the sight of God; forthwith the devil found an opportunity while the angels were absent and the devil led your mother astray to eat of the unlawful and forbidden tree. And she did eat and gave to me.

Chapter XXXIV

And immediately, the Lord God was wroth with us, and the Lord said to me: "In that thou hast left behind my commandment and hast not kept my word, which I confirmed to thee; behold, I will bring upon thy body seventy blows; with divers griefs shalt thou be tormented, beginning at thy head and thine eyes and thine ears down to thy nails on thy toes, and in every separate limb." These hath God appointed for chastisement. All these things hath the Lord sent to me and to all our race.

Chapter XXXV

Thus spake Adam to his sons, and he was seized with violent pains, and he cried out with a loud voice, " What shall I do? I am in distress. So cruel are the pains with which I am beset." And when Eve had seen him weeping, she also began to weep herself, and said: "O Lord my God, hand over to me his pain, for it is I who sinned."

And Eve said to Adam: "My lord, give me a part of thy pains, for this hath come to thee from fault of mine."

Chapter XXXVI

And Adam said to Eve: "Rise up and go with my son Seth to the neighborhood of paradise, and put dust on your heads and throw yourselves on the ground and lament in the sight of God. Perchance He will have pity upon you and send His angel across to the tree of His mercy, whence floweth the oil of life, and will give you a drop of it, to anoint me with it, that I may have rest from these pains, by which I am being consumed."

Chapter XXXVII

Then Seth and his mother went off toward the gates of paradise. And while they were walking, lo! suddenly there came a serpent and attacked and bit Seth. And as soon as Eve saw it, she wept and said: "Alas, wretched woman that I am. I am accursed since I have not kept the commandment of God." And Eve said to the serpent in a loud voice: "Accursed beast! how is it that thou hast not feared to let thyself loose against the image of God, but hast dared to fight with it?"

Chapter XXXVIII

The beast answered in the language of men: "Is it not against you, Eve, that our malice is directed? Are not ye the objects of our rage? Tell me, Eve, how was thy mouth opened to eat of the fruit? But now if I shall begin to reprove thee thou canst not bear it."

Chapter XXXIX

Then said Seth to the beast: "God the Lord revile thee. Be silent, be dumb, shut thy mouth, accursed enemy of Truth, confounder and destroyer. Avaunt from the image of God till the day when the Lord God shall order thee to be brought to the ordeal." And the beast said to Seth: "See, I leave the presence of the image of God, as thou hast said." Forthwith he left Seth, wounded by his teeth.

Chapter XL

But Seth and his mother walked to the regions of paradise for the oil of mercy to anoint the sick Adam: and they arrived at the gates of paradise, and they took dust from the earth and placed it on their heads, and bowed themselves with their faces to the earth, and began to lament and make loud moaning, imploring the Lord God to pity Adam in his pains and to send His angel to give them the oil from the "tree of His mercy."

Chapter XLI

But when they had been praying and imploring for many hours, behold, the angel Michael appeared to them and said: "I have been sent to you from the Lord — I am set by God over the bodies of men — I tell thee, Seth, thou man of God, weep not nor pray and entreat on account of the oil of the tree of mercy to anoint thy father Adam for the pains of his body.

Chapter XLII

"For I tell thee that in no wise wilt thou be able to receive thereof save in the last days."

When five thousand five hundred years have been fulfilled, then will come upon earth the most beloved king Christ, the son of God, to revive the body of Adam and with him to revive the bodies of the dead. He Himself, the Son of God, when He comes will be baptized in the river of Jordan, and when He hath come out of the water of Jordan, then He will anoint from the oil of mercy all that believe in Him. And the oil of mercy shall be for generation to generation for those who are ready to be born again of water and the Holy Spirit to life eternal. Then the most beloved Son of God, Christ, descending on earth, shall lead thy father Adam to Paradise to the tree of mercy.

Chapter XLIII

"But do thou, Seth, go to thy father Adam, since the time of his life is fulfilled. Six days hence his soul shall go off his body, and when it shall have gone out thou shalt see great marvels in the heaven and in the earth and the luminaries of heaven." With these words, straightway Michael departed from Seth.

And Eve and Seth returned bearing with them herbs of fragrance, *i.e.*, nard and crocus and calamus and cinnamon.

Chapter XLIV

And when Seth and his mother had reached Adam, they told him, how the serpent bit Seth. And Adam said to Eve: "What hast thou done? A great plague hast thou brought upon us, transgression and sin for all our generations: and this which thou hast done, tell thy children after my death, for those who arise from us shall toil and fail but they shall be wanting and curse us and say, All evils have our parents brought upon us, who were at the beginning." When Eve heard these words, she began to weep and moan.

Chapter XLV

And just as Michael the archangel had foretold, after six days came Adam's death. When Adam perceived that the hour of his death was at hand, he said to all his sons: "Behold, I am nine hundred and thirty years old, and if I die, bury me toward the sunrising in the field of yonder dwelling." And it came to pass that when he had finished all his discourse, he gave up the ghost.

Chapter XLVI

Then was the sun darkened and the moon and the stars for seven days, and Seth in his mourning embraced from above the body of his father, and Eve was looking on the ground with hands folded over her head, and all her children wept most bitterly. And behold, there appeared Michael the angel and stood at the head of Adam, and said to Seth: "Rise up from the body of thy father and come to me and see what is the doom of the Lord God concerning him. His creature is he, and God hath pitied him."

Chapter XLVII

And all the angels blew their trumpets, and cried: "Blessed art thou, O Lord, for thou hast had pity on Thy creature."

Chapter XLVIII

Then Seth saw the hand of God stretched out holding Adam, and he handed him over to Michael, saying: "Let him be in thy charge till the day of Judgment in punishment, till the last years when I will convert his sorrow into joy. Then shall he sit on the throne of him who hath been his supplanter."

And the Lord said again to the angels Michael and Uriel: "Bring me three linen clothes of byssus, and spread them out over Adam, and other linen clothes over Abel his son, and bury Adam and Abel his son."

And all the "powers" of angels marched before Adam, and the sleep of the dead was consecrated. And the angels Michael and Uriel buried Adam and Abel in the parts of paradise, before the eyes of Seth and his mother and no one else, and Michael and Uriel said: "Just as ye have seen, in like manner, bury your dead."

Chapter XLIX

Six days after, Adam died; and Eve perceived that she would die, so she assembled all her sons and daughters, Seth with thirty brothers and thirty sisters, and Eve said to all: "Hear me, my children, and I will tell you what the archangel Michael said to us when I and your father transgressed the command of God.

"On account of your transgression, our Lord will bring upon your race the anger of his judgment, first by water, the second time by fire; by these two, will the Lord judge the whole human race.

Chapter L

"But harken unto me, my children. Make ye then tables of stone and others of clay, and write on them all my life and your father's, all that ye have heard and seen from us. If by water the Lord judge our race, the tables of clay will be dissolved and the tables of stone will remain; but if by fire, the tables of stone will be broken up and the tables of clay will be baked hard."

When Eve had said all this to her children, she spread out her hands to heaven in prayer, and bent her knees to the earth, and while she worshiped the Lord and gave him thanks, she gave up the ghost. Thereafter, all her children buried her with loud lamentation.

Chapter LI

When they had been mourning four days, then Michael the archangel appeared and said to Seth: "Man of God, mourn not for thy dead more than six days, for on the seventh day is the sign of the resurrection and the rest of the age to come; on the seventh day the Lord rested from all His works."

Thereupon Seth made the tables.

www.ingramcontent.com/pod-product-compliance
Lightning Source LLC
LaVergne TN
LVHW041458070426
835507LV00009B/681